LEADERSHIP RE-THINK!

366 WAYS TO CLAIM AND POLISH THE LEADER WITHIN YOU

Stephen M. Gower, CSP
Lectern Publishing
P.O. Box 1065, Toccoa, GA. 30577

Best-Selling Author of: *"What Do They See When They See You Coming?"*

First Edition, Published 2007, By LECTERN PUBLISHING, P.O. Box 1065, Toccoa, GA 30577

Although the author and publisher have exhaustively researched all sources to ensure the accuracy and completeness of the information contained in this book, we assume no responsibility for errors, omissions, inaccuracies, or any other inconsistency herein. Any slights or mistakes are purely unintentional.

Other books by Stephen M. Gower, CSP include:

What Do They See When They See You Coming?

Like a Pelican in the Desert: Leadership Redefined

Perception: Make It Your Business

Mountains of Motivation

Think Like a Giraffe

Traveling By Detour: Living with Struggle and Surprise

Celebrate the Butterflies

The Kangaroo Factor

The Focus Crisis!

Have You Encouraged Someone Today?

More Books by Stephen M. Gower, CSP include:

The Art of Killing Kudzu: Management by Encouragement

The Missing Lynx: Public Speaking for High School Students

Zebra Dazzle: How to Build Stunning Teams

Advocacy Required: How to Transform Customers into Advocates

Upsize Selling

Stretchability: How to Build Your Agenda for Growth

smg@stephengower.com - 800-242-7404

DEDICATION

My normal routine is to dedicate a book to a professional speaker colleague, my wife, or a special friend. In this instance, I make an exception.

It is my honor to dedicate *Leadership Re-Think: 366 Ways to Claim and Polish the Leader Within You* to Heather Cowan.

Heather blesses our office with a spirit that is refreshing beyond the norm. She continues to bless me with insights into leadership that transcend my preconceptions about leadership. Every office-team should be so blessed as to have a Heather Cowan.

ACKNOWLEDGEMENTS

Modeling was very important to me when I was a child. Whether it was mud or clay, sand or tiny wood pieces, I enjoyed crafting models: an airplane, a sand castle, a pot, a pie.

Modeling continues to be an important part of my life. I must confess that, for the most part, I am now on the receiving end of modeling. I am the beneficiary of relationships with a cadre of leaders who have not only modeled stellar leadership skills, but have encouraged me to claim and polish the leader within me.

In particular, I would like to acknowledge, with a deep appreciation some of those persons who have sculpted a mold of leadership-excellence: Dr. Belle Wheelan, Dr. Wayne Livingston, Mr. Ron Seib, Mr. Ben Cheek, Mr. Roy Gaines, and Ms. Jeanette Jamieson.

If "the given" plus "the gathered" equals "the growth," (and it does), then I have gathered much from these men and women. My spirit of gratitude is authentic.

INTRODUCTION

This book is an invitation to think about the leadership-thoughts you think. It is a challenge to refuse to believe everything you do think, indeed a call to re-think!

If you think leadership is more about power than influence, re-think! If you think leadership is position-specific and not person-centered, re-think! If you think you are supposed to stay "up there," and not go "down there," re-think!

We have been led to believe that leadership is all about soaring. There are situations or occasions in which leaders must re-think their projects, re-think their team members, re-think their positions. A leader's journey is not always an upward soaring. Uppercase LEADERS are encouraged to work their way toward lowercase leaders, encouraging them to claim and polish the leader within themselves.

If you think leadership has more to do with infusing what you do not have than with releasing what you already have (and who you already are), re-think! If you think persons who choose to be leaders either start with something or nothing, if you do not think that each of us starts with something, then, re-think. If you think you can polish silver but not your leadership skills-set, re-think.

If you think leading others is more important than leading oneself, if you think that one can give what one does not have, re-think. If you think leadership starts at school, or at work, but not at home, re-think. If you think there are uppercase LEADERS, but not lowercase leaders, re-think. If you think management and leadership are the same thing, that imposition is stronger than inspiration, re-think.

If leadership is an elitist club, not an embracing culture, if you look within and sense you are on the out (side), then re-think. There is more of a leader within you than you ever imagined. Re-think about it!

*Leadership can equal the
extension of your personality
coming through in what
you do, specifically at the points
of your influence. Authentic
leadership will never invite you
to be who you are not.*

Leadership Re-Think!

1   § Leadership is not about laboring to insert into yourself what you do not have; leadership is about letting loose what is already within you, polishing, and polishing more.

2   § Leadership is not about a label; leadership is about a labor that equals an influence.

3   § There is more leadership potential within you than you can even began to comprehend.

4   § Genuine leadership will not ask you to be who you are not.

5 § Phoniness is apparent; it also smells.
  Authenticity is obvious; it is also stellar.

6 § Leadership is release, not implantation.
  Remember, you start with much more than
  nothing.

7 § Leadership talent and personality are
  inextricably related. Sadly, talent within
  you often goes unrecognized or undeveloped.
  The lack of recognition and the absence of a
  subsequent development do not mean that the
  talent is not there - within you.

There is already within each of us a leadership skills-set, perhaps very raw and initially obscure, that can be claimed and polished.

8   § Since leadership is more about influence, than power, when it comes to leadership potential, there is always something there (better worded, something within there) for each of us.

9   § When it comes to the development of leadership skills in general, and who can develop those skills in particular, the answer is not "only those who are born with them," or "only a few." The answer is: "there is a potential for influence within each of us that can be claimed and polished!"

Leadership Re-Think!

10   § Leadership has more to do with influence than power.

11   § Leadership is not an elitist club; leadership is an embracing culture.

12   § For sure, there are uppercase *LEADERS* and there are lowercase *leaders*, but the confines and limitations that many of us ascribe to leadership are, in reality not nearly as strict and narrow as we may portend.

13 § Potential minus practice equals the problematic. To hold marvelous potential for positive influence within you (and you do), and then to refuse to claim and polish that potential is a violation against yourself and your team.

14 § If leadership encompasses influence, and it does, then your circle of leadership is broad enough to include home, school, work, community!

Leadership Re-Think!

*Lead by your influence.
Occasionally you will
find it essential to talk!*

15 § Your words often whisper; your behavior often shouts!

16 § Often, it is what you do not think about that denies you the leadership (influence/inspiration) that you desire.

17 § The leadership clock runs non-stop; your influence-microphone and your influence-camera are always on.

18 § You may never know, or fully comprehend, the particular source or the broad scope of your influence.

Leadership Re-Think!

19   § Not all influence is positive influence.

20   § It is often an enigma, but oh so true - the
positive influence that took you years to build
can be tarnished, even destroyed, in a matter
of seconds.

21   § The artificial can irritate; the authentic
can inspire.

Leadership at it's strongest is inspiration, not imposition.

Leadership Re-Think!

22   § The force of leadership is often the
freedom it embraces.

23   § The spirit of imposition is demeaning
and destructive; the spirit of inspiration
is affirming and constructive.

24   § "Have to" rarely wins against "want to."

25   § Demand is inferior to desire; choice
trumps chore.

26 § Whereas inspiration is refreshingly the tool of leadership, imposition is often (and unfortunately) the instrument of management.

27 § The terms "leader" and "boss" do not seem to go together. In fact, they clash.

28 § Whereas inspiration can light a fire, imposition can backfire.

When your world wobbles, when stumbling, not soaring, seems to be your mantra, when your leadership feels shaky, find help.

29 § There is help within. The peace and presence
that you cannot figure out, that comes from
within, is Him!

30 § There is help at the point of perspective.
You have been there before (awkwardness).
You made it through then, why not now?

31 § There is help out there - your army of allies
(mentors, colleagues, counselors, friends,
family).

Leadership Re-Think!

32 § There is more help out there - your arsenal
of resources (trade magazines, books, DVD
and CD learning packages, the internet).

33 § The shakes (the struggle) have a strange way
of preparing one for the steady (the soaring).

34 § Help will often come at the point of surprise,
but it usually requires a prepared place.

35 § Ultimately, instead of sitting around and
waiting for happy endings, and instead of
sitting around waiting for a motivator, you
have to take responsibility for your actions.

*There can be a leadership-blessing
in a leadership-blemish.*

36   § Learning from your "where you have been," especially if it is an uncomfortable detour, can actually service your journey and assist you in polishing your leadership skills-set.

37   § Anticipate detours. The anticipation will lessen their sting.

38   § Accept the blemish of the detour. This is not the same thing as celebrating or even acquiescing. You are simply accepting (acknowledging) that "this is the way it now is" and asking "what do I now do?"

39 § Analyze what you can learn from the blemish, the detour. Nuggets of leadership-wisdom often follow on the heels of a detour.

40 § Apply what you learn. The analysis minus the application equals a leadership-aggravation and a leadership-waste.

41 § Appreciate, not the detour, but what the detour has taught you. Be grateful for leadership lessons-learned.

42 § To anticipate, accept, analyze, apply, and appreciate in the midst of leadership-detours is to soar beyond success.

The insinuation that leaders should perpetually suppress all of their emotions is fraught with error.

43 § The more "human" a leader projects herself/himself to be, the more likely she/he is to be respected.

44 § Leaders who choose to be vulnerable at points of hurt or disappointment are often respected as being strong, not weak.

45 § Be the leader you want to see.

46 § Staying in touch with your emotions can bless, not curse, a perspective of balance and a discerning spirit.

47   § The journey toward an acceptance of your feelings will facilitate within you a tendency to accept the feelings of others as well.

48   § Certain feelings mandate a leadership-perspective of distance before there is a response. A glance into possible, future consequences often has a way of altering leadership-perspective.

49   § Thinking before you speak says volumes!

Leader:
what you fear can bless
your leadership!

Leadership Re-Think!

50   § Delegating may help, not hurt.

51   § Failure can teach, not always torture.

52   § Restraint can trump impulsiveness.

53   § Your being open (even vulnerable) may
      unite your team; not divide it.

54 § Those who appear out to hurt you may be out to help you. (Unfortunately, the reverse is also true: those who appear out to help you may actually be out to hurt you.)

55 § Detours can deliver delightful surprises.

56 § Leaders: keep fear in balance. Fear can be an important arrow in the leader's quiver - calling for re-direction, perhaps even a halting. However, fear taken too far can equal an instrument that inflicts leadership-paranoia and may result in leadership-paralysis.

*Leadership has more to do
with the person than the place or
the position. Leadership is not an
elitist club, it is an embracing culture.*

57 § Leadership equals the combination of your attitudes and behaviors. Leadership (your influence/inspiration) can unfold wherever you are.

58 § Lead your life; lead your work! Make your difference!!

59 § Leadership is huge - but never so large as to exclude you.

60 § Read *You Don't Need A Title To Be A Leader* by Mark Sanborn.

61 § Leadership is encouragement, even caring enough to confront - you can do this.

62 § Leadership is often the construction of an idea, the implementation of an idea, and the nurturing of an idea - inviting team participation throughout the process - you can do this.

63 § Leadership is influencing and inspiring - you can do this.

Leadership is not "everything you are not." Leadership is "everything you are."

64 § Your entire "where you have been" can help you manufacture influence and create differences.

65 § Re-thinking leadership is about **you**.

66 § Remember, leadership is not as much about catching something on the outside and then releasing it. It is more about catching (and sculpting) something on the inside and then releasing it. (Re-think: catch and release.)

67 § How exciting is this? Your past (your experience) can influence their future (their experience yet to unfold).

68 § Think influence "upon" others - not influence "over" others.

69 § Underestimate yourself enough and you may eventually prove yourself right.

70 § Within your inner life cupboard there is a huge and stellar bundle of leadership experience - and leadership potential - yet to be explored.

When leaders think like managers, control is emphasized more than communication.

71 § If your team members think "control" when they see you coming (and not "communication"), then, you have some work to do.

72 § When "control" is your mantra, you are limiting, not enabling, your team members.

73 § Being open to "input from others" does not mean you do not have preferences as to idea and approach. Openness will not always equal agreement or acquiescence.

Leadership Re-Think!

74 § When your team members see you coming,
you want them to think "leader" not
"manager." The key lies within their
perception of you. How they perceive you
is critical!

75 § Leadership is reciprocal. Leadership
extended invites leadership returned.

76 § Act like a manager, you are likely to produce
managers. Act like a leader, you are likely
to produce leaders.

77 § Managers and leaders seem to operate within
a different time frame. Managers think in
terms of event; leaders think in terms of
process.

The more you learn about the thoughts you think, and their power over your leadership, the more you learn to filter and to respond appropriately to those thoughts.

78 § Leadership programmed within can equal
leadership thrust in an outwardly direction.

79 § The influence you have over yourself is huge.

80 § What you say to yourself, knowingly or
unknowingly, is supremely important. In
fact, it is more important than what you say
to others.

81 § The language you program into your head
and heart, informs and influences what you
say to others. It also affects your leadership.

82 § The thoughts you think are so important that you must be very careful about what you think. Specifically, do not believe everything that you think.

83 § Bless yourself, and your leadership, with this challenge: "There are times when I must re-think leadership."

84 § You cannot lead others if you cannot lead yourself.

Wise is the leader who teaches:
"If leadership is making a difference
(and it is), then there lies within
each of us a leader."

85   § Tradition has taught, incorrectly, that leadership flows in only one direction - downward. Leadership also flows in another direction - upward!! (In order to implement this genre of leadership, uppercase LEADERS may need to move downward.)

86   § Your influence upon those to whom you report is not merely wishful thinking; it equals reality.

87   § "Leading on the up" occurs when you take seriously your opportunity and responsibility to service the journey of your LEADERS.

88   § If encouragement is important to you, then why would encouragement not be important to them (your Uppercase LEADERS)?

89   § What is good for uppercase LEADERS is normally good for lowercase leaders.

90   § If you appreciate feedback, then why would they not appreciate feedback? (The way you send out your feedback is critical. You do not want to be perceived as condescending or excessively confrontational. A great suggestion, delivered ineffectively, can equal rejection.)

91   § "One" (Uppercase LEADER) can equal a very lonely number! The leader within you can help you service the journey of other leaders - as either an encourager or a teacher - or both.

When you start feeling sorry for yourself as a leader (either as LEADER or as leader), do not stay on the pot of pity too long. Do something!

Volunteering breeds leadership-influence with muscle! Volunteer - A rattle in your car may seem significant until you encounter someone who has no car. A small leak in your roof may seem highly problematic, until you encounter someone with no home.

204 § Volunteering with a charity-based, or not-for-profit organization, can yield huge dividends at the point of developing a positive leadership-influence.

205 § Volunteering will help you re-think your perspective.

206 § Choosing to volunteer will help you to re-think your priorities.

207 § Casting your influence as a volunteer can help keep you off the debilitating pity pot.

208 § When you receive support, encouragement, and especially a like mindedness, from those with whom (for whom) you volunteer, you are given a hint of what a relationship with those whom you lead can look like.

209 § Creating circumstances that take you away from yourself leads to something remarkable - you become more creative.

210 § Volunteering births gratitude; gratitude births a new vigor for a positive influence.

Re-think: "No looking back."

Leadership Re-Think!

211 § The leader who wants to soar beyond mere success, particularly at the point of influence, will indeed choose "to look back."

212 § Look back - to see what went well!

213 § What worked well in the past, might do so again in your leadership-future.

214 § Identify, set aside, and examine what helped build your positive influence in your past. This will assist you in duplicating or expanding your positive influence. (Examples: Specificity when affirming others; servicing your own journey; factoring perception into your leadership-equation.)

215 § Look back - to examine what went wrong!

216 § What went wrong in your leadership-past
is likely to continue unless there is an
addressing and an adjustment.

217 § Identify, set aside, and examine what had a
negative impact on your leadership. This
will assist you in eliminating or minimizing
factors that contributed to a less than desired
influence. (Examples: impatience, procrasti-
nation, failure to model your expectations.)

Re-think about it: A key leadership (influence/inspiration) issue may not be time-management as much as it is energy-management! Be a good steward of your energy!!

218 § At the expense of energy-management, many focus on time-management.

219 § What you do with your energy may be just as important, if not more important, than what you do with your time.

220 § What you eat can go to your head - and steal your energy. Monitor closely the foods you eat, the beverages you drink, and the medicines you take. Consult your doctor.

221 § Your energy-level informs the level of your influence.

222 § Ask yourself: "Is this worth the energy I am spending on it? Is the return on the investment of my energy positive or negative?"

223 § Fatigue clouds the vision, mutes the desire, dwarfs the discipline!

224 § Energy exhaled requires energy inhaled! If you want the energy to craft a positive influence, then service yourself well!

***Leadership is often painful before
it becomes satisfying - even fun!***

225 § Out of the crucible of struggle can emerge the discovery of excitement.

226 § Learning to ponder leadership in both broader and startling perspectives equals a journey that is often laced with detours.

227 § Often, we learn our leadership-lessons from our "where we have been."

228 § The road to leadership is often paved with much awkwardness and many zigs and zags - but you can do this - just identify your starting place - it is on the inside.

229 § A substantive call for leadership will mandate a look within before it beckons an outward journey.

230 § The ground that equals a leadership re-thinking often becomes shaky before it can become solid.

231 § Learning the lesson is often worth the price. Lessons learned can lead to an exploration and celebration of the remarkable relationship between individual team member choices and stellar team-performance patterns.

Stellar leaders recognize the polarity that embraces "the quick" and "the quiet."

232 § A leader can be quick with temper; this is destructive.

233 § A leader can be quick as in "keen" or "sharp;" this is constructive.

234 § You and those you influence benefit when you manage (control) the quick temper and lead (communicate) with a mind that is quick in the "keen" sense of the word.

235 § A leader can be quiet as in "retreat and pout;" this is destructive.

236   § A leader can be quiet as in "retreat and reflect;" this is constructive.

237   § You and those you influence benefit when you manage (control) and limit your moments on the pot of pity and lead (influence/inspire) from a "retreat and reflect" perspective.

238   § Stack the "quick and quiet" odds in your favor - and in the favor of your positive influence.

Leaders are not grounded in "expectation" - they not only do more than is expected, they often do what is not expected at all.

Leadership Re-Think!

239 § Leaders create a difference that is positive when they transcend expectation.

240 § When leaders move beyond expectation, and does not expect HEADLINE CREDIT, that is leadership.

241 § Leaders soar beyond success when their labor is persistently more important than their label.

242 § The responsibility to lead others should not be shaped (specifically) by the expectations of the others.

243 § You are a leader in life when you refuse to be defined by expectations.

244 § Re-think expectations! Expectations can provide structure, they can also present inappropriate and debilitating limits.

245 § "That is exactly what I expected" may not prove to be a compliment.

Leadership Re-Think!

*Leadership is about the person,
not the position!*

246 § When position is a prerequisite for leadership, the masses are omitted.

247 § You can lead (influence/inspire) wherever you are.

248 § Leadership is the inertia of a person (an extension) at the point of an influence that is positive.

Leadership Re-Think!

249 § When leadership is defined by the position, and not by the person, that can equal form minus force!

250 § When a state trooper is called to an accident, he is called to exhibit leadership; when a mother is asked to be a mentor, she becomes a leader; when a teenager becomes a patrol leader in his boy scout troop, he should emphasize "leader" in "patrol leader;" even a brand new scout (or cub scout) can exhibit a positive influence - holding absolutely no position!

251 § The tug to help can be stronger than the call for recognition; even the very young can experience the pull to help.

252 § There are more leaders than you have ever imagined. You are one of them.

The potential for leadership, creating a beneficial influence upon others, lies within you. The issue is not mere discovery; it is release.

253 § Leadership is a team captain who leads his team toward a state championship and that same captain mentoring a six year old who wants to learn how to throw a touch down pass or become a quarterback.

254 § The leadership ranks welcome a grandmother who teaches the power of a positive influence to her grandchild by exampling positive influence herself.

255 § We misunderstand the power and fulfillment of leadership when we impose limits upon it.

256 § If you think leadership belongs to the few,
then it is time to re-think.

257 § Leadership is fun, why be selfish with it?

258 § The difference-creators are many - a world
full! You are one of them. *Claim and Polish the
Leader within You.*

259 § Far too long our definition of leadership
has been far too narrow.

Leadership Re-Think!

> # *You are in the*
> # *manufacturing business!*

260 § Leadership is the creation of differences, the manufacturing of an influence upon others that is positive.

261 § If you want to enhance the leadership you bring to others on a daily basis, then recognize and utilize your capacity to manufacture influence and create (inspire) differences.

262 § The leadership power, place, and purpose does not merely belong to others. *Claim and Polish the Leader within You!* For some, this will be a huge leap.

263 § Just as there are two types of stress - positive (eustress) and negative (distress), so are there two genres of influence - positive (what you need to seek) and negative (what you must avoid).

264 § What you manufacture does matter!

265 § You can influence others for help, or for hurt.

266 § The issue is whether or not you are influencing in a positive manner. You are manufacturing and delivering influence. The question is: What type of influence are you crafting and sending out toward others?

*Leadership will equal
G-R-I-D-L-O-C-K
when you refuse to
Go Beyond!*

267 § Go beyond **Rut**. Think **Renewal**. Renewal requires vision, structure, and accountability.

268 § Go beyond **Inadequacy**. Think **Initiative**. Initiative necessitates the first step.

269 § Go beyond **Dread**. Think **Delight**. Delight will often catch you by pleasant surprise - particularly where preparation meets awkwardness.

270 § Go beyond **Laziness**. Think **Responsibility**. Responsible decisions will birth positive influence.

271 § Go beyond **Obligation**. Think **Opportunity**. Choice trumps chore.

272 § Go beyond **Confrontation**. Think **Affirmation**. On occasion, you must care enough to confront. At other times, when confrontation seems easier than affirmation, you must re-think.

273 § Go beyond **Keeping**. Think **Sharing**. Is it more about you or them? (For related reading on G-R-I-D-L-O-C-K, read *Like a Pelican in the Desert* by SMG.)

Sometimes, leadership is confrontational.

274 § Confrontation need not mean that you care less; it could mean that you care more.

275 § Exhibit confrontation like the donut. The area of your concern is the donut hole. You encompass the hole when appropriate, with positive comments. It is beneficial if these positive comments take the shape of the donut - if they come before and after the donut hole.

276 § This "donut" concept can certainly be taken too far. Caution: Do not dilute the donut hole (the essence of the confrontation, or better worded the addressing).

277 § What you say may not equal what is heard!
Verify the intended receipt of the message:
"Now, what did you just hear me say?"

278 § Ponder this leadership question: "Are you
attacking a person or addressing an issue?"

279 § Confrontation is more effective if that is not
all someone hears from you!

280 § If they sense that you "catch and translate"
when they are doing wrong, but never "catch
and translate" when they are doing well, you
may not only have a perception-problem
(their perception); you may also have an
influence-problem (your influence).

To claim and polish the leader within you is to discover (and rediscover) the strengths within you - and then to sculpt those strengths.

281 § Although both strength-sculpting and weakness-chiseling are important, there is wisdom in leading from you strengths!

282 § Strengths undiscovered and strengths undeveloped equals strengths wasted.

283 § Humility can be a strength - but not if you know it. Stating "I am humble" sends a conflicting message.

284 § Admission of limitation (vulnerability) can equal a strength.

285 § The strength of doing something well, and the enjoyment of doing that very thing, go hand in hand - indeed complement each other.

286 § You do not have to broadcast your strengths; they speak for themselves.

287 § Your arsenal of resources is not only on the outside; your arsenal of resources will include what is on the inside - particularly at your influence points of character and competency.

Claiming and polishing the leader within you is a one-two punch - attitude and behavior.

288   § "Claiming" is based at the point of attitude.

289   § To claim the leader within you equals: an attitude of acceptance - even affirmation, recognition - even resolution, enthusiasm - even excitement, inspiration - even intent.

290   § To claim is not to polish. "Claiming" is a first step, in developing a positive influence.

291   § "Polishing" is grounded at the point of behavior.

292 § To polish the leader within you equals:
a behavior of pursuit - even practice;
engaging - even excelling; starting - even
sculpting; succeeding - even soaring!

293 § To polish is not to claim. Polishing is folly
where there is no claiming.

294 § The form (claiming) plus the force (polishing)
equals the fulfillment (of a positive influence).

Take a second look at the issue of leadership and compliments.

295 § How you receive compliments may be just as important as how you give compliments.

296 § Quickly passing off another's compliment has consequences.

297 § Taking the compliments of others lightly (too lightly) can discourage their attempts at positive influence. It can be perceived by them as rejection. For many, it takes a tremendous amount of courage to compliment another person.

298 § How you receive compliments influences how others receive compliments.

299 § Perceived rejection (the consequences of a trite reply or no reaction at all) can be replaced by a positive response.

300 § Try: "I appreciate your comments today. I have been working to improve in this area. Your specific encouragement is meaningful to me because I have been wondering if indeed I was improving."

301 § Your influence - your capacity to receive a compliment - can equal a great gift, really two gifts: one for you (encouragement) and one for them (a sense of "leading back"), and a sense of doing their part at the point of sharing their positive influence (their leadership).

*Leadership is not so much
talking, it is "exampling."
Beneficial exampling will not
emerge from a superficial spirit;
it emerges from a spirit
of sincerity.*

302   § In leadership, authenticity is primary!

303   § Eloquence is insignificant when compared to exampling. Eloquence is irrelevant if it is merely for show.

304   § Eloquence minus authenticity equals external (and eventually internal) aggravation.

305   § Your well-expressed words of influence could have a short shelf-life. However, your positive example (or lack of it) is powerful beyond years.

306 § The example you express is under specific
   scrutiny when you are under pressure.

307 § This bears repeating: You are always imaging.
   Your microphone and your camera are
   perpetually in the "on" position.

308 § When you make an example-mistake, admit it.
   Even the way you deal with your example-
   mistakes "examples."

When you cannot see them because you are in the way, there is a huge leadership vacuum.

309 § When there is a problem, and you cannot see it, that is a problem - now you have two problems.

310 § Unfortunately, most of us have practiced "how to fool ourselves" for decades.

311 § The approach (trap) of tricking yourself into thinking "only a certain way" - and then manipulating the facts so that they become "your facts" - is manipulation not leadership. It is a brutal habit - detrimental to self, detrimental to team.

312 § Moving beyond the trap of standing in one's own way requires admission (attitude) and action (behavior).

313 § Transcending the prison or confining situation of standing in the way of your leadership-goals may require you to seek professional help.

314 § Read *Leadership and Self-Deception* by The Arbinger Institute.

315 § Sometimes, influence will ask you to get out of the way.

Evaluation has two gears, not one.
Integrity seeks to wear
one face, not two.

316 § The tendency to evaluate others and the reluctance (refusal) to be open to evaluation of the self by others borders on hypocrisy.

317 § By identifying conflict within yourself (the tension between "evaluations are good for them" and "I do not benefit when they evaluate me"), you are taking a remarkable first step.

318 § Change within you breeds change within others. Openness on your part can set the stage for openness on their part.

Leadership Re-Think!

319 § Introspection prepares us for being more open.

320 § We profit when we isolate and monitor any conflict between beliefs and behavior. Such activity can lead to a remarkable Leadership Agenda for Growth.

321 § Integrity expected is most profound when it extends out from integrity exampled.

322 § The strength to face a hint of hypocrisy ("I have a tendency to evaluate them but a reluctance to have them evaluate me.") will enable you to be embraced by confidence, even touched by courage.

Joy trumps happiness!

323 § As you lead, remember that happiness is grounded in circumstances while joy is rooted in choices.

324 § Joy redefines accomplishment.

325 § Happiness is predictable; joy will catch you by pleasant surprise.

326 § Joy is very illusive where there is a void of leadership-integrity.

327 § Healing, harmony, and a refreshing sense of hope are three of joys' habitats.

328 § Joy looks outside itself. Joy touches who many will refer to "The One who blesses us with a Peace that passeth understanding."

329 § Joy is authentic leadership's mighty "igniter," its faithful rudder! Leaders touched with joy are rarely bound by circumstance.

When someone says to you: "You make me feel a certain way," re-think!

330 § You cannot be held responsible for making a person feel a certain way.

331 § Ultimately your team members have control over their feelings, unless they choose to acquiesce control of their feelings to you.

332 § You cannot motivate them - but you can create a motivational environment where they are more likely to motivate themselves.

333 § You cannot make them feel angry or guilty - but you can for sure create an environment where they are more likely to feel that way.

334 § Choices create circumstances; choices create feelings.

335 § If you choose to allow them to get away with holding you responsible for their feelings, that is your choice.

336 § There comes a time for saying: "Wait a minute; you are giving me too much credit." or, "Wait a minute; should I take all the blame for this awkward situation?" Leadership mandates the question: "Who is (are) responsible here?"

Leaders: Re-think recognition/awards. They can be dangerous!

337 § Do your homework. If you plan for a public event for purposes of recognition for a team member, be sure it is merited. Make certain others who might also deserve recognition are not omitted.

338 § Make a big deal out of a big deal. Do not mail an award; hand deliver it.

339 § When presenting the award, investigate. Discover all you can about what makes this recipient special and his/her efforts so stellar.

340 § Be timely. Normally, distance will diminish impact. (Remember: on rare occasions a "We continue to appreciate what you did last year. We benefit from it daily and think of you often!" will pay huge dividends.)

341 § When appropriate, surprise the recipient by asking the recipient's family to be present.

342 § Take a picture of the event. Frame it. Hand deliver it.

343 § Catch your team members with pleasant surprises.

Leadership is a privilege.

344 § Leadership is not a burden; it is a blessing.

345 § Leadership is not an obtrusive chore; it is an inviting and enabling choice.

346 § Ultimately, leadership is to be enjoyed, not endured. Endurement births resentment; enjoyment can birth a movement beyond success.

347 § Leaders are to serve, not merely to be served.

348 § Leaders are to help - not impeed, and not
      micro-lead. "Constriction" should not be
      utilized in describing a leader. "A Passion
      to Empower" can be helpful in depicting
      stellar leaders.

349 § Respect the opportunity to be respected.

350 § Leadership is honorable! That is - when
      leaders are honorable.

Re-think "the I's have it."
Leadership is all about "the I's."
In this case "I" is not a first
person pronoun.

Leadership Re-Think!

351 § Introspection: Leading the self, *claiming and polishing the leader within you*, is essential. Study yourself, grow yourself, celebrate yourself.

352 § Invitation: An army of allies and an arsenal of resources are out there to help you grow at the point of leading yourself - and others.

353 § Involvement: Leadership is either "do, drop, or delegate." In many instances, it is "delegate." Involve your team members in not only the action-stage, but in the idea-stage. Your team members will benefit when they feel they own, at least to a degree, the inventory of the ideas.

354 § Instruction: Refuse to assume that your team members know what to do. Again, do not micro-lead, but do present your team members with the information they need to get the job done.

355 § Interaction: Be out there with them. Do the mundane. Example expectation.

356 § Inspiration/Influence: They will look to you. Encourage the team.

357 § Integrity: Loyalty/commitment expected must be "exampled" by loyalty/commitment extended.

Re-think motivation!
Seek to motivate yourself and
strive to create a motivational
environment for your team members.

358 § Redefine motivation. Stop waiting for happy endings. Stop waiting for a motivator. Think like this: "Motivation is an inside thing." (For further information on motivation, read *Mountains of Motivation* by SMG.)

359 § Think: "Attention, about face, forward march!" Allow someone or something to garner your attention. Let the attention-getting lead to an "about face." March toward growth. (Examples: where "about face" can unfold: anger, excessive confrontation, and generalized affirmation!)

360 § Think about the thoughts you think. Do not "think yourself" into defeat. Value your mind as a mold and hold vessel.

361 § Whether hurtful habits or helpful habits are the issue, growth comes by way of focus. Appreciate focus loss as: concentration collapse, determination dwindling, thought tyranny. View hurtful habits as motivation-blockers.

362 § Detours will get in your motivation-way. Expect and manage detours.

363 § Massage the environment of those you lead by servicing their journey. Service is an action verb.

364 § Value clarity of purpose, commitment to effort, consistency of effort, and the cyclical nature of personal growth.

"What makes you smile?"
- That is a great question!

365 § Surround yourself with smile starters!
Children's toys, circus animals, special
pictures can elicit smiles. Display for yourself
pictures of you taken at an awkward age or in
a bizarre moment.

366 § Smiles often emanate out from a solid inner
strength. If what they see when they see you
coming as their leader equals nothing but
frowns, grimaces, and frustration, then you
have a leadership-problem. If what they see
when they see you coming as their leader, at
least occasionally, reveals smiles, laughter, and
joy, then you have a leadership-opportunity.

Surround yourself with team members blessed with a sense of humor. Smile at a stranger, welcome smiles from another. Normally, a day without a smile hurts the team.

Leadership is hope, but it is more than mere hope. Leadership is grounded in strategy. Strategy's rudder equals the marriage between your internal mandates and the team/project mission.

Leadership-strategy routinely unfolds in the shape of: this is What we are going to do; this is Why we are going to do it; this is How we will do it! The earlier the team is involved in the process, the better. You want the team to feel as if they have an ownership in the inventory of the ideas and in the implementation.

Strategy is fueled by the leader's integrity; strategy falls apart where there is no integrity. Your internal mandates (your personal mission) trump team/project mission. If there is conflict between your internal voice and the team mission, the team project will never soar.

*Leadership transcends desire
and encompasses focus! Focus equals
the intensity of concentration,
the increase of determination,
and the integrity of thought.*

Now, how to claim and polish the leader within you is up to you. It will require a Leadership Re-Thinking.
I wish you well!

For information about:
Leadership Re-Think!
366 Ways to Claim and Polish the Leader Within You
at quantity discounts, and for information
on Mr. Gower's books, keynote speeches,
seminars and consulting,
call (800) 242-7404
or fax (706) 886-0465.

www.stephengower.com
smg@stephengower.com

STEPHEN M. GOWER, CSP, is respected worldwide as **The Perception Professional**. He works with organizations who want to lead change. He brings to the forefront an exploration and celebration of the remarkable relationship between individual team member choices and stellar team performance patterns. His unique blend of enthusiasm, experience, and content produces stunning results at the point of the passion behind change. His *What Do They See When They See You Coming*? book is recognized as the signature work on perception across the globe.

Earning a bachelor's degree from Mercer University and his master's degree from Emory University, Stephen has given more than 5,000 presentations and is a best selling author of seventeen books. As a Certified Speaking Professional, Stephen M. Gower will transfer knowledge in a powerful, pervasive, and long-term fashion. Routinely, Stephen's inspiration and information lead to an on-going implementation. Experience "The Perception Professional" - Stephen M. Gower, CSP.

Made in the USA
Coppell, TX
11 March 2025

46937727R10098